Our Favori
Kid-Approved recipes

Copyright 2024, Gooseberry Patch
Previously published under ISBN 978-1-62093-208-7
Cover: Oven-Baked Chicken Fingers (page 35)

French toast sticks are yummy dunked in syrup,
but try topping 'em with fruit jam, apple butter,
whipped cream, cinnamon-sugar or even warm pie filling!

French Toast Sticks

6 slices bread
2 eggs
1/2 c. milk
1/4 t. sugar

1/4 t. cinnamon
1 T. oil
Garnish: maple syrup, powdered
    sugar or cream cheese

Cut each bread slice into 3 or 4 sticks using kitchen scissors. Beat eggs with a whisk in a bowl and then mix in milk, sugar and cinnamon. Dunk each bread stick into mixture one at a time, letting the bread soak up the egg. Spread oil on a hot griddle or skillet. Add bread sticks and cook over medium heat for 2 to 3 minutes. Squish with a potato masher gently so each piece is crisp in the center without burning the crust. Flip with a spatula when crisp on one side; repeat on the other side. Dip in maple syrup, sprinkle with powdered sugar or spread with cream cheese.

This recipe originally came from England. It gets
its name because the egg looks as if it's
peeking out of a hole!

Toad in the Hole

Serves 2 to 4

4 slices bread
non-stick vegetable spray

4 eggs
salt and pepper to taste

Spray both sides of bread with non-stick vegetable spray and place on cutting board. Cut a hole in the middle of each slice of bread using the juice glass and keep the circles you cut out. Toast bread slices and circles in a skillet over medium heat for 2 minutes on each side. Crack an egg into the hole of each bread slice and cook another 2 to 3 minutes, or until eggs are set. Use a spatula to flip and cook second side one to 2 minutes. Sprinkle with salt and pepper, if you like. Place completed toads-in-the-hole on serving plates and top each with a bread circle so it looks like your "toad" is peeking out!

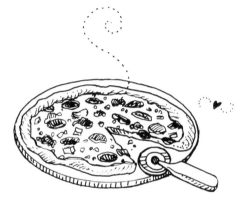

No peeking! Every time you open the oven door,
heat escapes and the pizzas take longer to cook.

Rise & Shine Pizzas

Serves 4

4 ready-to-use mini pizza crusts
1-1/2 cups shredded Cheddar
    cheese, divided
1/2 lb. brown & serve breakfast
    sausage links, cut into
    bite-size pieces

non-stick vegetable spray
6 eggs, beaten
salt and pepper to taste
Optional: 1/4 cup pizza sauce

Place crusts on an ungreased baking sheet. Sprinkle with half the cheese. Cook sausage in a sprayed skillet over medium heat until browned, about 3 minutes. Put sausage on a plate. Drain fat from skillet. Beat eggs with a whisk in a mixing bowl. Sprinkle with salt and pepper. Pour eggs into skillet. Turn heat to low. Scramble eggs by gently turning with a spatula until they're cooked but not dried out. Spoon sausage and egg onto crusts. Add a little pizza sauce, if you like. Sprinkle on the rest of the cheese. Bake at 400 degrees for 10 to 12 minutes, until cheese melts.

Crack eggs one by one into a separate small bowl, not directly
into the mixing bowl. That way, if you find a "bad egg"
it will be easy to throw away.

Get Up & Go Cookies

Makes 18 cookies

1/2 c. butter, softened
3/4 c. sugar
1 egg, beaten
1 c. all-purpose flour
1/4 t. baking soda

2 c. multi-grain flake cereal
1/2 to 3/4 c. precooked bacon, chopped
1/2 c. golden raisins

Blend butter and sugar together in a mixing bowl until light and fluffy. Stir in egg. Mix flour and baking soda together in another bowl; stir into butter mixture. Stir in cereal, bacon and raisins. Drop by rounded teaspoonfuls onto an ungreased baking sheet, 2 inches apart. Bake at 350 degrees for 15 to 18 minutes, until golden. Cool on baking sheet for 2 minutes. Lift off cookies with a spatula to finish cooling on a wire rack.

Spoon batter into cookie cutters to make fun pancake shapes! Give it
a try using hearts, stars or gingerbread man cutters.
Add a clip-on style clothespin to the cutter so it is easy
to lift off a hot griddle or skillet.

Mom & Me Chocolate Chip Pancakes

Serves 2

1/3 c. raspberry jam
1/2 c. frozen raspberries, thawed
1 T. butter
1 T. water
1 c. biscuit baking mix

1/2 c. milk
1 egg, beaten
3 T. semi-sweet chocolate chips
non-stick vegetable spray
Optional: whipped topping

Combine jam, berries, butter and water in a small saucepan. Cook over low heat until thickened and bubbly. Keep warm. Stir biscuit mix, milk, egg and chocolate chips together in a mixing bowl. Pour batter by 1/4 cupfuls onto a sprayed griddle or skillet over medium heat. Cook on one side until bubbles start to pop. Flip and continue cooking other side until golden. Drizzle with spoonfuls of warm raspberry sauce. Add a dollop of whipped topping, if you like.

Berry-delicious fruit straws...slide strawberry and banana slices onto drinking straws, then put one in each glass. Scrumptious!

Banana-Berry Smoothies

1 ripe banana, sliced
1/2 c. strawberries, sliced
1 c. vanilla yogurt, divided
1 c. milk, divided

1 c. orange juice, divided
Optional: 1/2 c. orange sherbet,
 divided

The night before, mix banana and strawberry slices in a bowl. Divide the mixture between 2 small plastic bags. Spoon 1/2 cup yogurt into each bag, on top of fruit. Press bags closed. Freeze bags overnight. In the morning, break up one frozen bag of fruit with your hands. Pour it into a blender along with 1/2 cup milk and 1/2 cup juice. Add 1/4 cup sherbet, if you like. Blend until smooth, with an adult's help. Pour into a glass to serve. Repeat to make a second smoothie, or save the second bag in the freezer for another day.

Coney dogs are named for Coney Island in New York City.
A hundred years ago, Coney Island was the most
popular amusement park in the US!

All-American Coney Dogs

Serves 4 to 6

1/2 lb. ground beef
1/4 c. onion, chopped
1 clove garlic, minced
8-oz. can tomato sauce
1/4 c. water

1/2 t. chili powder
4 to 6 hot dogs
4 to 6 hot dog buns
Garnish: shredded cheese, pickle
relish, catsup, mustard

Crumble ground beef in a skillet. Add onion and garlic. Stir well, using a wooden spoon. Cook over medium heat until no pink remains and onion is soft. Drain off the fat, using a colander. Stir in tomato sauce, water and chili powder. Simmer over medium heat for 10 minutes, stirring occasionally. Cover hot dogs with water in a small saucepan. Simmer over medium heat until they're hot. Place hot dogs in buns, using tongs. Spoon sauce over them. Add your favorite toppings.

Use a serrated bread knife to cut sub sandwiches in half...
it won't mash the tasty fillings inside. Always keep your hands
on top of the knife!

Zesty Sub Sandwiches

4 submarine buns
2 tablespoons butter, softened
4 leaves lettuce
2 tomatoes, thinly sliced
1/4 lb. sliced deli salami

salt and pepper to taste
1/4 lb. sliced Swiss cheese
1/4 lb. sliced deli ham
2 T Italian salad dressing
1/4 t. garlic salt

Slice buns in half lengthwise. Spread butter on the cut side of the bun bottoms. Layer lettuce, tomato and salami slices on the buttered bread. Sprinkle with a little salt and pepper. Add cheese and ham. Sprinkle with salad dressing and garlic salt. Place top halves on buns to make sandwiches. Cut in half, if you like.

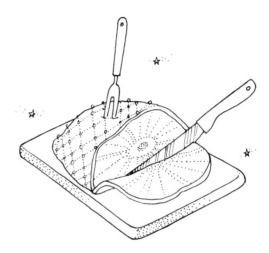

Make your roll-up unique! Everyone can add their favorite fillings...
ham & pineapple, taco meat & salsa, corned beef
& Swiss cheese or pepperoni & mushrooms.

Ham & Cheese Roll-Ups

Serves 2 to 4

3 to 4 slices deli ham
4-oz. tube refrigerated crescent
    rolls

3 to 4 t. mustard
1/4 c. shredded Cheddar cheese

Cut ham into small pieces using kitchen scissors. Unroll crescent rolls on an ungreased baking sheet. Pull apart the dough triangles on the dotted lines. Spoon a little mustard onto each triangle. Sprinkle each roll with one tablespoon cheese and one tablespoon ham. Roll triangles up, starting from the long side. Place on an ungreased baking sheet. Bake at 350 degrees for 11 to 13 minutes or until rolls are golden.

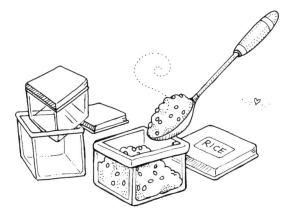

When you want to refrigerate leftovers, let them
cool down a bit before placing in the refrigerator.

Tex-Mex Taco Joes

Makes 25 sandwiches

3 lbs. ground beef, browned
    and drained
16-oz. can refried beans
10-oz. can enchilada sauce
1-1/4 oz. pkg. taco seasoning mix

16-oz. jar salsa
25 hot dog buns, split
Garnish: shredded Cheddar
    cheese, shredded lettuce,
    chopped tomatoes, sour cream

Place beef in a slow cooker. Stir in beans, enchilada sauce, seasoning mix and salsa. Cover and cook on low setting for 4 to 6 hours. To serve, fill each bun with 1/3 cup beef mixture; garnish as desired.

While cooking on the stove, don't step away to play a game
or talk on the phone. Keep your eyes on what's cookin'!

Ultimate Grilled Cheese Sandwiches

Makes 4 servings

8 slices white bread
8 slices American cheese
8 t. butter, softened

4 t. grated Parmesan cheese,
   divided

Assemble bread and cheese to make 4 sandwiches, enclosing 2 slices cheese in each. Spread outsides of sandwiches with butter; place on an ungreased baking sheet. Bake, uncovered, at 400 degrees for 8 minutes. Sprinkle with half of the Parmesan cheese. Flip sandwiches; sprinkle with remaining Parmesan. Return to oven for 6 to 8 minutes, until golden.

Before using a knife to slice the apple, it's always a good idea to have an adult close by to help out or answer questions.

Apple & Turkey Sandwiches

Serves 4

2 T. jellied cranberry sauce
2 T. mayonnaise
8 slices sourdough bread
1 lb. deli turkey, thinly sliced

1 Granny Smith apple, cored,
  peeled and thinly sliced
1 c. shredded Cheddar cheese

Mix together cranberry sauce and mayonnaise; spread evenly over bread slices. Arrange bread on an ungreased baking sheet. Divide turkey evenly among bread. Top turkey with apple slices; sprinkle with cheese. Broil until cheese is melted and golden.

An apron is a terrific way to keep spills and stains off clothes.

BLT Tuna Sandwiches

Makes 4 sandwiches

7-oz. pkg. white tuna, drained
3 T. bacon bits
1/4 head lettuce, shredded
1 tomato, diced

1/2 to 1 c. mayonnaise
salt and pepper to taste
8 slices multi-grain bread, toasted
Garnish: dill pickle spears

Combine tuna, bacon, lettuce and tomato with enough mayonnaise to achieve desired consistency. Add salt and pepper to taste. Pile tuna mixture high on 4 bread slices. Top with remaining bread and serve with pickle spears.

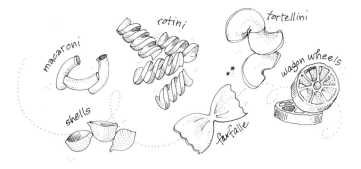

Shape up! Wagon wheels, seashells, bowties...try all the great pasta shapes in this recipe!

Lucky Noodle Bowl

Serves 2

2 c. water
3/4 c. veggies like mushrooms, peas and spinach, finely chopped or shredded

3/4 c. cooked chicken, chopped
3-oz. pkg. chicken-flavored ramen noodles
Optional: soy sauce

Pour water into a saucepan. Add the veggies and chicken. Bring to a bubbly boil over medium heat. Unwrap noodles and set aside the seasoning packet, for now. Carefully place the whole block of noodles in the boiling water. Cook for 3 minutes, until noodles are tender. Turn over noodles once or twice with the spoon so they'll cook evenly. Turn down the heat a little if it's boiling too hard. Remove pan from heat. Open the seasoning packet and sprinkle the seasoning over the noodles. Stir to mix all the ingredients. Ladle into 2 soup bowls. Add a little soy sauce, if you like, and share with a friend.

Remember not to leave boxes or bags of groceries out on the floor where they can trip up a fast-moving cook!

Taco Chili Bake

Serves 6

1-1/4 c. biscuit baking mix
1/2 c. milk
15-oz. can chili with beans
1-1/2 c. shredded Cheddar
    cheese, divided

1/4 t. paprika
Garnish: sour cream, shredded
    lettuce, chopped tomatoes,
    sliced black olives, sliced
    green onions

Stir biscuit mix and milk together to make a soft dough. Spread half of dough in an ungreased baking pan with a spatula. Top with chili and 3/4 cup cheese. Add the rest of the dough over cheese in 6 big spoonfuls. Sprinkle with paprika. Bake at 400 degrees for about 25 minutes, until golden on top. Cut into squares. Sprinkle with the rest of the cheese and add your favorite toppings.

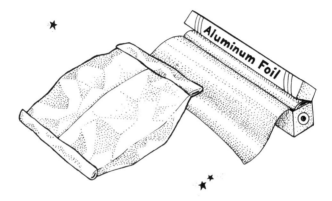

The foil packages can be grilled outdoors on a medium-high covered BBQ grill for 9 to 10 minutes. Have an adult do this.

Grilled Pepper Steak Packets

Serves 2

1/2 lb. boneless beef sirloin,
    cut into strips
1/2 t. garlic powder
1/8 t. pepper
1 c. instant rice, uncooked
1 green pepper, cut into strips

1/2 c. broccoli flowerets
1/2 sweet onion, sliced
1/2 c. teriyaki sauce
4 ice cubes
1 c. water

Place half of beef in center of 2 18-inch pieces of foil. Sprinkle with garlic powder and pepper. Spoon rice around beef. Top with pepper strips, broccoli and onion. Add 1/4 cup sauce and 2 ice cubes to each packet. Fold foil up on sides, then double-fold top and one end. Pour 1/2 cup water into each packet. Double-fold other end to seal. Place on baking sheet. Bake at 450 degrees for 12 to 15 minutes. Open very carefully to let hot steam escape. Stir rice before serving.

For a delicious cold picnic food, chill baked chicken
well, then wrap up the pieces in wax paper and
put them in a picnic cooler.

Oven-Baked Chicken Fingers

Serves 6

1 c. Italian-flavored dry bread
    crumbs
2 T. grated Parmesan cheese
1/4 c. oil

1 clove garlic, minced
6 boneless, skinless chicken
    breasts

Preheat oven to 425 degrees. Heat a large baking sheet in the oven for 5 minutes. Meanwhile, combine bread crumbs and cheese in a shallow dish; set aside. Combine oil and garlic in a small bowl; set aside. Place chicken between 2 sheets of heavy-duty plastic wrap. Flatten chicken to 1/2-inch thickness, using a meat mallet or rolling pin; cut into one-inch-wide strips. Dip strips into oil mixture; coat with crumb mixture. Coat preheated baking sheet with non-stick vegetable spray and arrange chicken on prepared baking sheet. Bake at 425 degrees for 12 to 14 minutes, turning after 10 minutes, until golden and chicken is no longer pink in the center.

Be sure to put each ingredient back in the cupboard or fridge as soon as you finish using it.

Cowboy Beans & Rice

Serves 4

1-1/2 c. boiling water
1-1/2 c. instant rice
1 beef bouillon cube
1 T. oil
1 onion, chopped
1 green pepper, chopped

2 15-oz. cans pinto beans,
  drained
3/4 c. barbecue sauce
4 hot dogs, sliced
Optional: corn chips

Pour boiling water over rice and bouillon cube in a bowl. Cover with
a lid for 5 minutes. Combine oil, onion and green pepper in a large skillet.
Cook over medium heat for 3 to 5 minutes, stirring occasionally, until
veggies are soft. Stir in beans, sauce and hot dogs. Fluff rice with a fork
and stir it into skillet. Simmer over medium heat for 5 to 7 minutes, until
hot and bubbly.

Give your pizza a funny face! Tomato slices become
eyes and a green pepper slice makes an open mouth...
add a mushroom slice for the nose!

Funny Face Pizzas

16.3-oz. tube large refrigerated
    biscuits
non-stick cooking spray
1 c. pizza sauce
2 c. shredded mozzarella cheese

Garnish: pepperoni slices,
    mushroom pieces, crunchy
    snack twirls or other favorite
    pizza toppings

Separate biscuits and flatten each to a 6-inch circle. Place biscuits on
sprayed baking sheets. Spoon some pizza sauce onto each biscuit. Spread
almost to the edges. Sprinkle cheese over the sauce. Add toppings like
sliced pepperoni, sliced veggies and crunchy snack twirls to create faces.
Bake at 375 degrees for 10 to 15 minutes, until crusts are deep golden
on the bottom and cheese is bubbly.

This recipe uses cooked pasta. Ask an adult for help when draining the pasta, since the steam could cause a burn.

Twistin' Tomato Pasta

Serves 4 to 6

1/4 c. olive oil
1/2 c. onion, chopped
2 cloves garlic, minced
1-1/2 lbs. boneless, skinless
   chicken, cut into 2-inch cubes

2 t. Italian seasoning
28-oz. can stewed tomatoes
8-oz. pkg. rotini pasta, uncooked
Garnish: grated Parmesan cheese

Heat oil over medium heat in a large skillet. Add onion and garlic. Cook and stir for 3 to 4 minutes. Stir in chicken and seasoning. Cook until chicken is no longer pink inside, about 10 minutes. Add tomatoes with juice. Turn heat down to low and simmer while you cook the pasta. Fill a stockpot with water and bring to a boil. Add pasta and cook for 8 to 10 minutes, stirring so it doesn't stick. Drain pasta in a colander. Stir pasta into sauce. Sprinkle with Parmesan cheese.

Try 'em for breakfast! Scrambled eggs, grated cheese, sausage or
bacon make these quesadillas worth
getting out of bed for.

Easy Cheesy Quesadillas

Serves 2 to 4

1 c. cooked chicken, shredded
2 T. onion, chopped
1/4 c. diced green chiles
1/4 c. salsa or taco sauce
4 flour tortillas

1 c. shredded Monterey Jack
  cheese
Optional: additional salsa, sour
  cream and guacamole

Combine chicken, onion, chiles and salsa in a deep skillet. Cook chicken mixture over medium heat for 5 minutes, or until onions are soft. Stir mixture occasionally. Place 2 tortillas side-by-side on an ungreased baking sheet. Spoon half the chicken mixture onto each tortilla. Sprinkle cheese over chicken mixture and top with remaining tortillas. Bake at 350 degrees for about 15 minutes, or until cheese is melted. Serve with additional salsa, sour cream and guacamole, if you like.

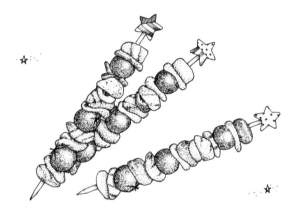

Make it an all-on-sticks meal! Start with fresh veggie cubes
to skewer and dunk in creamy ranch dressing. For dessert, serve your
favorite frozen fruit pops!

Wiki-Wiki Chickie Kabobs

1-1/2 lbs. boneless, skinless
    chicken, cut into 1-inch cubes
20-oz. can pineapple chunks,
    drained
2 green peppers, cut into 1-inch
    squares

1 pt. cherry tomatoes
10-oz. bottle sweet-and-sour
    sauce
non-stick vegetable spray
Optional: cooked rice

Arrange chicken, pineapple, green peppers and tomatoes on skewers.
Brush sauce over kabobs. Place kabobs on a sprayed broiler pan. Place
pan under a heated broiler and broil for 2 to 3 minutes. Turn kabobs over
and brush sauce on the other side. Broil for another 2 to 3 minutes, until
chicken is golden and no longer pink inside. Serve kabobs on a scoop of
cooked rice, if you like.

Keep floors free of slippery spots by having a
damp cloth handy to wipe up spills.

Hamburger Crunch

Serves 6 to 8

2 lbs. ground beef
1 T. onion, minced
2 10-3/4 oz. cans tomato soup
1 t. chili powder

4 c. corn chips
8-oz. pkg. shredded Cheddar
    cheese

Brown ground beef and onion together in a large skillet over medium heat; drain. Stir in soup and chili powder. Spread in an ungreased 13"x9" baking pan; top with corn chips. Bake, uncovered, at 350 degrees for 20 to 25 minutes. Remove from oven; sprinkle with cheese. Bake for an additional 5 minutes, until cheese melts.

It's tater time. Potatoes used to be grown for only their decorative flowers...people thought the potato itself was poisonous. Today, they're the world's most popular veggie!

Baked French Fries

Serves 2 to 4

3 potatoes   salt to taste
1 T. oil   non-stick vegetable spray

Scrub potatoes using a vegetable brush. Cut potatoes into 1/2-inch thick sticks by first slicing potatoes and then stacking the slices, about 3 at a time, to cut into sticks. Toss potato sticks with oil and salt in a mixing bowl until evenly coated. Place on a sprayed baking sheet in a single layer. Bake at 475 degrees for 15 minutes. Flip fries with spatula carefully. Continue to bake about 25 minutes, or until golden and crispy. Sprinkle with additional salt to taste and serve.

Spoons that are made of metal can get hot quickly
when stirring food on the stove. It's best to use
wooden or plastic spoons.

Spicy Fried Apples

Makes 6 servings

1-1/2 lbs. Granny Smith apples, cored and cut into wedges	1/4 t. cinnamon
	1/4 t. nutmeg
1-1/2 T. sugar	1/4 c. bacon drippings or butter

In a bowl, toss apples with sugar and spices. Heat drippings or butter in a large skillet over medium-high heat. Add apples to skillet. Cook until tender and golden, turning to cook on all sides, about 10 minutes. Serve warm.

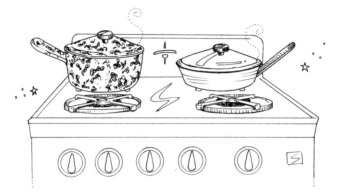

If you have a little brother or sister close by, remember that hot baking sheets or pans should be kept where they can't be reached.

Best-Ever Stuffing Balls

Serves 6

10 c. dry bread crumbs or
   1 loaf day-old bread, cubed
1/2 c. butter
1 c. celery, finely diced
1 onion, finely diced
10-3/4 oz. can cream of
   mushroom soup

1 t. dried sage
1 t. dried thyme
1 t. salt
1/2 c. fresh parsley, chopped,
   or 1/4 c. dried parsley

Place bread crumbs or cubes in a large bowl. In a skillet over medium heat, melt butter. Sauté celery and onion until tender; add celery mixture to bowl. Add soup and seasonings; mix well. Form mixture into 12 to 14 balls. Place in a greased 13"x9" baking pan; cover with aluminum foil. Bake, covered, at 350 degrees for 25 minutes.

A baked sweet potato is an easy side just about everyone will love. Bake at 375 degrees until tender, about 40 to 45 minutes, then top with a little butter and cinnamon-sugar.

Peachy-Keen Sweet Potatoes

Serves 10

2 lbs. sweet potatoes, peeled
    and cubed
1 c. peach pie filling

2 T. butter, melted
1/4 t. salt
1/4 t. pepper

Place sweet potatoes in a slow cooker that has been sprayed with non-stick vegetable spray. Add remaining ingredients; mix well. Cover and cook on low setting for 5 to 7 hours, until potatoes are tender when pierced with a fork.

Always wear an oven mitt when opening the oven
to check on your food.

Simply Delicious Potatoes

Makes 10 to 12 servings

32-oz. pkg. frozen diced potatoes, thawed
26-oz. can cream of chicken soup
16-oz. container sour cream
8-oz. pkg. shredded sharp Cheddar cheese
8-oz. pkg. pasteurized process cheese spread, diced

Combine all ingredients in a slow cooker; mix well. Cover and cook on high setting for about 2 hours, until hot and bubbly.

Brighten a dinner plate with edible fruit and veggie garnishes...
try carrot curls, pineapple spears or kiwi slices.

Cheryl's Corn Fritters

Serves 6

2 c. corn
1 egg, beaten
1-1/2 t. sugar
2 T. butter, melted and divided

1/3 t. salt
1/8 t. pepper
1/4 c. all-purpose flour
1/2 t. baking powder

Combine corn, egg, sugar, one tablespoon butter, salt and pepper. Add flour and baking powder; mix well. Heat remaining butter in a medium skillet over medium-high heat; drop batter by 1/4 cupfuls. Cook for 2 to 3 minutes per side, or until golden.

Before beginning any recipe, wash your hands in lots of
warm, soapy water, then dry well.

Beefy Potato Cakes

1 T. oil
1 onion, chopped
2 c. mashed potatoes

1 c. roast beef, shredded
salt and pepper to taste

Heat oil in a large skillet over medium heat; add onion and cook until tender. Transfer onion to a medium bowl; mix with potatoes, beef, salt and pepper. Form into 8 patties; return to skillet and cook over medium-high heat until golden on both sides.

For extra zing, top Baked Mac & Cheese with salsa,
nacho cheese dip or chopped green chiles.

Baked Mac & Cheese

Serves 3 to 4

1 c. elbow macaroni, uncooked
1/2 c. pasteurized process cheese
    sauce
2 hot dogs, chopped

1 t. grated Parmesan cheese
4 buttery round crackers,
    crushed
salt and pepper to taste

Fill a stockpot with water and bring to a boil. Add macaroni and cook for 8 to 10 minutes, stirring so it doesn't stick. Drain, using a colander. Heat cheese sauce in microwave for one minute. Combine cooked macaroni, cheese sauce, chopped hot dogs and Parmesan in an ungreased casserole dish using a wooden spoon. Top with cracker crumbs and sprinkle with salt and pepper to taste. Bake at 350 degrees for 10 minutes.

It's a good idea to leave the lid slightly off center while simmering or
boiling...keeps liquid from boiling over
and you can easily keep an eye on it.

Herbed Butter Noodles

12-oz. pkg. wide egg noodles,
   uncooked
2 T. butter
1/4 c. fresh parsley, minced

1 t. fresh rosemary, minced
1/2 t. salt
1/4 t. pepper

Cook noodles as package directs; drain and keep warm. Place remaining ingredients in a skillet over low heat. Stir until butter melts and mixture is well blended. Add noodles to skillet; toss to coat well. Serve immediately.

Can't remember if you've already tried a recipe?
Draw a little smiley face in the page's margin...
you'll remember that it was a hit!

Sweet Ambrosia Salad

Makes 8 to 10 servings

20-oz. can pineapple chunks,
    drained
14-1/2 oz. jar maraschino
    cherries, drained
11-oz. can mandarin oranges,
    drained

8-oz. container sour cream
10-1/2 oz. pkg. pastel mini
    marshmallows
1/2 c. sweetened flaked coconut

Combine fruit in a large bowl; stir in sour cream until coated. Fold in marshmallows and coconut; cover and chill overnight.

Add a few drops of food coloring to
the pudding for a splash of color!

Fruit Trifle Salad

Serves 10 to 12

6 oranges, peeled and sliced
3 bananas, sliced
3 c. blueberries
2 c. seedless grapes
3 c. strawberries, halved

3.4-oz. pkg. instant vanilla
    pudding mix
1-3/4 c. milk
3/4 c. sour cream
1 t. orange zest

In a large glass bowl, layer all of the fruit in order listed above. For the topping, combine pudding mix and milk. Beat for one to 2 minutes. Beat in sour cream and orange zest. Serve with fruit salad.

Lunch is the perfect time to practice setting the table...
your family is sure to appreciate the help! Just remember,
forks go on the left, knives and spoons on the right.

Creamy Ranch Macaroni Salad

Serves 8 to 10

16-oz. pkg. medium shell pasta,
    uncooked
3/4 c. onion, chopped
1/2 c. celery, chopped
1 c. fresh Italian parsley, chopped

1 c. sour cream
1-oz. pkg. ranch salad dressing
    mix, divided
1 c. mayonnaise
1/2 c. shredded Cheddar cheese

Cook shells according to package directions; drain and rinse with cold water. Set aside. Combine onion, celery and parsley in a large bowl; add shells and toss together. Add sour cream and half the salad dressing mix; stir well. Add mayonnaise and remaining dressing mix; stir again. Toss with Cheddar cheese.

Twisty bread sticks are a tasty go-with for lunch or dinner. Brush
refrigerated bread stick dough with a little beaten
egg and dust with Italian seasoning, then pop
in the oven until toasty.

Creamy Pretzel Salad

Serves 10 to 12

1/2 c. butter
1 c. sugar, divided
3 c. pretzels, broken
8-oz. pkg. cream cheese, softened

8-oz. container frozen whipped
topping, thawed
20-oz. can pineapple tidbits,
drained

Melt butter in a saucepan over medium heat; stir in 1/2 cup sugar until dissolved. Place pretzels in an ungreased 13"x9" baking pan; pour butter mixture over top. Bake at 350 degrees for 10 minutes; let cool. Remove pretzel mixture from pan and break into pieces. Mix together remaining sugar, cream cheese, whipped topping and pineapple; stir in pretzel pieces. Chill.

For a delicious, healthy side that practically cooks itself, fill
aluminum foil packets with sliced fresh veggies. Top with seasoning
salt and two ice cubes, seal and bake at
450 degrees for 20 to 25 minutes, until tender.

Mozzarella & Tomato Salad

Makes 8 servings

8 tomatoes, chopped
1/2 c. olive oil
pepper to taste

16-oz. pkg. shredded mozzarella
  cheese
10 sprigs fresh basil, torn

In a large serving bowl, combine all ingredients; toss to coat. Cover and refrigerate for 30 minutes before serving.

Wash all fruits and vegetables before eating.
Use just clear, clean water and no soap.

Sunflower Strawberry Salad

Makes 6 servings

2 c. strawberries, hulled
   and sliced
1 apple, cored and diced
1 c. seedless green grapes,
   halved

1/2 c. celery, thinly sliced
1/4 c. raisins
1/2 c. strawberry yogurt
2 T. sunflower seeds
Optional: lettuce leaves

Combine fruit, celery and raisins. Stir in yogurt. Cover and chill one hour. Sprinkle with sunflower seeds just before serving. Spoon servings over lettuce leaves, if desired.

Serve up individual portions of Summertime Egg Salad in
edible bowls! Hollow out fresh green, yellow or red peppers
and fill 'em up with egg salad for a quick and tasty lunch.

Summertime Egg Salad

Makes about 4 servings

3-oz. pkg. cream cheese, softened
1/4 c. mayonnaise
3/4 t. dill weed
6 eggs, hard-boiled, peeled
   and chopped
1/4 c. sliced black olives
2 T. onion, chopped
1/4 c. celery, chopped
1/2 t. salt

Mix all ingredients together; chill in refrigerator before serving.

Graters are sharp...go slowly while grating
the carrot for this salad.

You're-the-Chef Salad

1 cucumber, peeled
1 red or yellow pepper
1 carrot, peeled
1/2 lb. deli smoked ham, turkey
    or chicken
4 eggs, hard-boiled and peeled

1 c. cherry tomatoes
1 head romaine lettuce, chopped
1 to 2 c. shredded Cheddar cheese
1 to 2 c. croutons
Garnish: favorite salad dressings

Slice cucumber and pepper using a paring knife. You could also use mini cookie cutters to cut out shapes, if you like. Grate carrot using the largest-holed section on your grater. Place in a bowl. Cut ham, turkey or chicken and hard-boiled eggs into separate bowls using kitchen scissors. Remove stems from cherry tomatoes and place them in a bowl. Place lettuce, cheese and croutons in separate bowls. Set up all the bowls of ingredients, along with your choice of dressings, salad-bar style on the table. Let everyone make their own salad!

If you open the oven door to take a peek,
close it quickly to keep the oven hot.

Pumpkin Muffins

Makes one dozen

1 c. plus 2 T. brown sugar, packed
   and divided
1/2 c. butter, melted
1-1/2 c. canned pumpkin
1/4 c. milk
2 eggs, beaten

2 c. all-purpose flour
1-1/2 t. baking powder
1/4 t. baking soda
1/2 t. salt
2 t. pumpkin pie spice
Optional: 1/2 c. raisins

Place 2 tablespoons brown sugar in a cup and set aside for the topping. Whisk the rest of the brown sugar, butter, pumpkin, milk and eggs together in a mixing bowl. Mix the rest of the ingredients in another mixing bowl. Pour in pumpkin mixture and stir just until flour mixture is moistened. Spoon batter into 12 paper-lined muffin cups, filling almost to top. Sprinkle with the brown sugar in the cup. Bake at 400 degrees for about 20 minutes, until muffin tops spring back when pressed lightly. Cool muffins in pan for 10 minutes. Remove from pan. Serve warm, or place on a rack to finish cooling.

On family game night, serve bread sticks crossed
like a tic-tac-toe game!

Pepperoni Pizza Breadsticks

Serves 2 to 4

10-oz. tube refrigerated
    garlic bread sticks
1 c. pizza sauce, divided

4-oz. pkg. pepperoni slices
3/4 c. shredded mozzarella cheese
non-stick vegetable spray

Place bread sticks in a single layer on a lightly sprayed baking sheet.
Spread about a spoonful of sauce on each bread stick. Top each with
4 to 5 slices pepperoni and sprinkle with mozzarella cheese. Bake at
375 degrees for 8 to 10 minutes, or until bread sticks are golden. Heat
remaining pizza sauce in the microwave until warm. Serve with bread
sticks for dipping.

Have some fun! Before baking, it's so easy
to twist pretzel dough into your initials,
a heart or X's and O's!

Sweet Pretzel Twists

Makes one dozen

11-oz. tube refrigerated bread
    sticks
2 T. butter, melted

1-1/2 T. sugar
1/2 T. cinnamon

Separate bread sticks and roll each one into an 18-inch rope. Shape each rope into a circle, overlapping ends by 4 inches. Twist ends together and fold over to form a pretzel shape. Place pretzels in a single layer on an ungreased baking sheet. Brush each with butter and then sprinkle with sugar and cinnamon. Bake at 350 degrees for 15 to 18 minutes.

Hot muffin tins can ruin a countertop. Be sure to set them on a wire cooling rack or potholder to cool.

Mom's Applesauce Muffins

Makes 12 to 16 muffins

1/2 c. butter, softened
1 c. sugar
1 egg, beaten
1 c. applesauce
1 t. cinnamon

1/2 t. ground cloves
1 t. baking soda
1/4 t. salt
2 c. all-purpose flour
1 c. raisins

Combine all ingredients; stir until moistened. Fill lightly greased muffin cups 3/4 full; sprinkle with Crumb Topping. Bake at 350 degrees for 25 to 30 minutes.

Crumb Topping:

1/2 c. butter
3/4 c. all-purpose flour
3/4 c. quick-cooking oats,
    uncooked

1/2 c. brown sugar, packed
2 t. cinnamon

Blend all ingredients until crumbly.

Remember...it's a good idea to get your tools out and make sure you have all the ingredients before starting.

Anytime Cheesy Biscuits

Makes about 1-1/2 dozen

2 c. biscuit baking mix
1/2 c. shredded Cheddar cheese
2/3 c. milk

1/4 c. margarine, melted
1/4 t. garlic powder

Combine first 3 ingredients and stir together until a soft dough forms; beat vigorously for 30 seconds. Drop dough by rounded tablespoonfuls onto an ungreased baking sheet; bake at 450 degrees until golden, about 8 to 10 minutes. Whisk margarine and garlic powder together; spread over warm biscuits.

When making muffins or sweet bread, stir just enough
to mix wet and dry ingredients...12 strokes is plenty!
The batter may be a little lumpy, but that's okay.

Blueberry Bread

Makes one loaf

1 c. sugar
3 c. plus 2 t. all-purpose flour,
    divided
1 t. salt
4 t. baking powder

1 egg, beaten
1 c. milk
2 T. butter, melted
juice of 1/2 lemon
1 c. blueberries

Sift together sugar, 3 cups flour, salt and baking powder in a bowl. Add egg, milk and butter. Do not beat; mix with a wooden spoon. Add lemon juice. Toss blueberries with 2 teaspoons flour; fold into mixture. Spread in a greased 9"x5" loaf pan and bake at 350 degrees for one hour.

Serve the dip in a round bread loaf! Just cut off the top,
pull out the bread inside and spoon in the dip.

Cheesy Pot-o'-Gold Dip

Serves 6 to 8

non-stick vegetable spray
6 to 8 spinach-flavor flour tortillas
3/4 c. chicken broth
1 to 2 T. Dijon mustard

1 T. cornstarch
2 c. shredded sharp Cheddar
cheese

Cut tortillas with a cookie cutter (or cut into wedges with a knife). Spray lightly with vegetable spray and place on an ungreased baking sheet. Bake at 375 degrees for 10 to 15 minutes, until crisp. Set aside to let cool. Pour broth into a saucepan. Bring to a boil over high heat. Turn heat down to low. Stir mustard and cornstarch together. Add to hot broth along with cheese. Cook until cheese melts completely. Keep stirring with a whisk until dip is smooth. Serve warm dip with tortilla chips.

Place some pretend "pickle chips" next to the sandwich.
Carefully peel a kiwi fruit and cut thin slices
with a paring knife.

"Grilled Cheese" & *Surprise Fries*

1 pound cake loaf from
  the bakery
12-oz. container white frosting
yellow and red food coloring

2 apples, cored and peeled
1 t. cinnamon-sugar
non-stick vegetable spray
1 tube red decorating gel

Cut 2 slices of pound cake, 1/2-inch thick. Toast and let cool. Stack slices
and cut in half diagonally. Stir one drop each of yellow and red coloring
into 1/2 cup frosting until it's orange like cheese. Spread frosting on cake
slices. Gently press together to form sandwich halves. Put on sandwich
plate and set aside. Cut apples into sticks with a knife or crinkle cutter.
Sprinkle lightly with cinnamon-sugar. Place on a sprayed baking sheet.
Bake at 400 degrees for 8 to 12 minutes, until apples are softened.
Arrange "fries" on plate next to "sandwich." Squeeze a blob of red
decorating gel onto plate for "catsup." Serve without giggling.

Keep foods tasty and safe...don't leave any food
sitting out more than 2 hours.

Broccoli Trees & Tuna Dip

Serves 6

8-oz. pkg. light cream cheese,
    softened
1/2 c. light mayonnaise
2 T. onion, finely chopped
1 t. dried parsley
1/2 t. dill weed

1/2 t. pepper
12-oz. can tuna, drained
    and flaked
1 bunch broccoli, cut into
    bite-size flowerets

Blend cream cheese and mayonnaise in a mixing bowl until smooth.
Stir in onion, parsley, dill weed and pepper. Add tuna and mix well. Chill
until serving time. Scoop dip into a serving bowl and place on a platter.
Arrange broccoli "trees" around the bowl.

Try using milk, dark or even white chocolate bars.
You might like them all!

Ooey-Gooey S'mores Puffs

Makes 8

8-oz. tube refrigerated crescent
   rolls
8 marshmallows
1-1/2 oz. milk chocolate candy
   bar, broken into squares

cinnamon to taste
non-stick vegetable spray
1/4 c. powdered sugar
1 to 3 T. milk

Unroll dough and separate into 8 triangles. Place a marshmallow and a
chocolate square at the wide end of each triangle. Sprinkle with a little
cinnamon. Roll up triangles around marshmallow and chocolate, starting
at the wide end. Tuck the bottom under and pinch the seams to seal
tightly. Arrange puffs in a sprayed round pan. Bake at 375 degrees for
10 to 15 minutes, until golden. Turn out onto a serving plate. Mix
powdered sugar and one tablespoon milk, adding more milk as needed
to make a runny icing. Drizzle over puffs and serve warm.

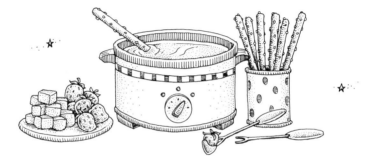

Fondue is a super sleepover treat...ask friends to bring along their favorite dippers like marshmallows, pretzel rods, strawberries and bananas to share.

Deliciously Dippable Fondue

Serves 6 to 8

1 c. chocolate chips
4 T. milk
pineapple, pear and apple slices
marshmallows

brownie and angel food
    cake cubes
pretzel sticks for skewers

Combine chocolate chips and milk in a microwave-safe bowl. Cook in microwave for one minute on high. Stir, then microwave for another 30 seconds. Skewer fruit, marshmallows or cake on the pretzel sticks and serve.

Ask for help with the oven and keep an eye on these little pizzas...the broiler cooks much faster than the oven!

Bagel Pizzas

Serves 4 to 6

4 bagels, sliced in half
8 T. pizza or
   spaghetti sauce

1/2 c. shredded mozzarella cheese
favorite pizza toppings
Optional: 1 t. Italian seasoning

Place each bagel half on a baking sheet. Spread one tablespoon of sauce on each bagel half. Sprinkle cheese evenly on top of the sauce. Add your favorite toppings and Italian seasoning, if you like. Broil bagels for 5 to 7 minutes, or until cheese is melted and golden.

Tortilla chips can be found in fun colors. Mix up a bowl of
yellow and orange ones for Halloween, or try combining
red and blue for the 4th of July!

Fiesta Nachos

Serves 4

1/2 lb. ground beef
1 t. chili powder
1 t. cumin
1/2 c. onion, chopped
10-oz. pkg. tortilla chips

2 c. shredded Cheddar cheese
1/2 c. tomato, chopped
1/4 c. black olives, chopped
Garnishes: salsa, sour cream
   and guacamole

Crumble ground beef in a skillet. Add seasonings and chopped onion and stir well. Cook beef and onion over medium heat until no pink remains and onion is soft. Drain using a colander. Layer half of tortilla chips, seasoned beef and cheese in an ungreased casserole dish. Add tomato and olives. Repeat until all ingredients are used. Bake at 375 degrees for 10 to 20 minutes, or until cheese is melted. Serve warm with salsa, sour cream and guacamole.

Coat your spoon with non-stick vegetable spray before
stirring sticky ingredients like honey...you can even
use it to coat your hands!

Teddy Bear Honey Munchies

Makes 15 servings

3-oz. pkg. ramen noodles
5 c. bite-size sweetened graham
   cereal squares
3 c. bear-shaped graham crackers
1 c. dry-roasted peanuts

1 c. raisins
1/3 c. butter
1/3 c. honey
1 t. orange juice
1/2 t. cinnamon

Crush ramen noodles; reserve seasoning packet for another use. In a large bowl, toss together noodles, cereal, crackers, peanuts and raisins; set aside. Combine remaining ingredients in a microwave-safe cup. Microwave on high, stirring after 15-second intervals, until well mixed and butter is melted. Pour over noodle mixture; toss to coat well. Spread onto ungreased rimmed baking sheets. Bake at 375 degrees for 10 minutes, stirring once. Cool before serving; store in an airtight container.

Start an electric mixer on the slowest speed, then turn it up as the recipe instructs. A rubber spatula is handy for scraping down the batter from the sides of the bowl.

Chocolatey Lava Cakes

1-1/3 c. semi-sweet chocolate
   chips
1/2 c. butter
1/2 t. vanilla extract
1/2 c. sugar

1/4 t. salt
3 T. all-purpose flour
4 eggs
1 T. baking cocoa
Optional: candy-coated chocolates

Place chocolate and butter in a microwave-safe bowl. Microwave on high for 30 seconds at a time until melted. Stir until smooth. Stir in vanilla. Mix sugar, salt and flour in a small bowl. Stir into chocolate mixture. Beat with an electric mixer on medium. Add eggs, one at a time, and beat on high for 4 minutes. Chill until cold. Grease top and 8 cups of a muffin tin lightly with butter. Sprinkle with cocoa and shake off any extra cocoa. Pour batter by 1/4 cupfuls into muffin cups. Bake at 375 degrees for 10 to 11 minutes, until cakes are set on outside and gooey inside. (Don't overbake them!) Carefully turn out onto dessert plates and serve warm.

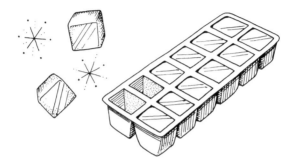

To crush ice cubes, place them in a heavy-duty plastic freezer bag and tap them gently with a rolling pin.

Lemon Shake-Up

Serves 1

1 lemon, halved
3 T. sugar

1-1/4 c. ice, crushed
3 T. water

Squeeze juice from lemon halves into a tall shaker container with a tight-fitting lid. Add sugar, enough ice to fill shaker 2/3 full and enough water to cover ice. Cover tightly and shake until sugar dissolves. Pour lemonade over lemon halves in a tall glass.

How about a caterpillar sundae? Place 3 scoops of
ice cream in a banana split dish...add cherry eyes
and licorice-whip antennae.

Ice Cream Sundaes

Serves 2

1 pt. favorite ice cream
caramel, chocolate or
    marshmallow ice cream
    topping
4 orange sections or 4 peach
    slices

jellybeans, gumdrops or candy-
    coated chocolates
2 maraschino cherries

Scoop ice cream and place a scoop in each of 2 glasses. Drizzle ice cream
with toppings. Top with another scoop of ice cream. Insert 2 fruit slices
in each scoop for "ears." Make a funny face with candies and cherries.
Add a long spoon to each glass and share with a friend!

Tighten the lid on the blender to keep your milkshake
from splattering everywhere!

Jungle Malt

2 c. milk
2 scoops vanilla ice cream

2 t. malted milk powder
2 ripe bananas, sliced

Combine all the ingredients in a blender. Blend on medium-high speed until smooth. Pour into 2 tall glasses. Add straws and share with a friend!

Containers made of metal or aluminum foil will cause sparks
in the microwave, so always use microwave-safe dishes.
Ask an adult to help you choose one.

Marvelous Caramel Bars

Makes one dozen

32 caramels, unwrapped
5 T. milk
1 c. quick-cooking oats, uncooked
1 c. all-purpose flour
3/4 c. brown sugar, packed
1/2 t. baking soda
1/4 t. salt
1/2 c. butter, melted
non-stick vegetable spray
1/2 c. semi-sweet chocolate chips
1/2 c. chopped walnuts

Combine caramels and milk in a microwave-safe bowl. Microwave on high setting for 1-1/2 to 2 minutes until melted, stirring occasionally. Mix oats, flour, brown sugar, baking soda and salt in a separate bowl. Stir in butter. Press half of oat mixture into a sprayed baking pan. Bake at 350 degrees for 8 minutes. Remove from oven; sprinkle with chips and nuts. Pour caramel mixture over top. Crumble the rest of the oat mixture and sprinkle it over top. Bake for 12 minutes more, until lightly golden. Cut into squares while still warm.

An apple peeler makes quick work of peeling apples!

Apple-Cinnamon Turnovers

Serves 6 to 8

3 apples, cored, peeled and diced
1 c. brown sugar, packed
3 T. all-purpose flour
3/4 t. cinnamon
1/4 t. nutmeg

2 8-oz. tubes refrigerated
   crescent rolls
2 T. milk
3/4 c. powdered sugar

Mix diced apples with brown sugar, flour, cinnamon and nutmeg. Separate crescent rolls on the dotted lines and place half of them on an ungreased baking sheet. Spoon one to 2 tablespoons of apple mixture in center of each crescent roll. Top each with another triangle of dough. Seal edges of dough together using a fork to crimp. Bake at 350 degrees for 12 to 15 minutes. Whisk milk and powdered sugar together until smooth. Drizzle glaze over each turnover while still hot.

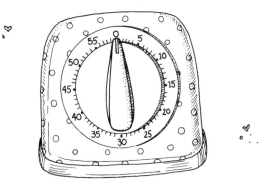

Be sure to set a timer for baking time for
yummy, not burned, cookies!

Snickerdoodle Cookies

Makes 20 cookies

1 c. butter
1-1/2 c. sugar
2 eggs, beaten
1 t. vanilla extract
2-3/4 c. all-purpose flour

2 t. cream of tartar
1 t. baking soda
2 T. sugar
2 t. cinnamon

Mix butter and 1-1/2 cups of sugar together in a large mixing bowl. Add beaten eggs and vanilla. Combine flour, cream of tartar and baking soda in another mixing bowl. Add flour mixture to the butter mixture a little at a time until the dough is blended and no flour is left in the bottom of the bowl. Combine remaining sugar and cinnamon with a fork in a cereal bowl. Roll dough into balls and toss in cinnamon-sugar. Place on an ungreased baking sheet. Bake at 400 degrees for 8 to 10 minutes, or until cookies are puffy and edges are golden. Cool on a wire rack 5 minutes.

Turn your hollowed-out watermelon from this recipe into a beat-the-heat cooler! Just fill with crushed ice and juice boxes.

Melonberry Lemonade

Serves 2 to 4

6 c. watermelon, cubed
   and seeded
1/2 c. raspberries

1 c. water
1/2 c. sugar
1/2 c. lemon juice

Combine watermelon, raspberries and water in a blender. Ask an adult to help out. Blend until smooth. Pour through a strainer into pitcher. Push liquid through with a rubber spatula when draining slows down. Stir sugar and lemon juice into strained mixture until sugar dissolves. Chill about 30 minutes or serve over ice.

INDEX

INDEX

Our Story

Back in 1984, we were next-door neighbors raising our families in the little town of Delaware, Ohio. Two moms with small children, we were looking for a way to do what we loved and stay home with the kids too. We had always shared a love of home cooking and making memories with family & friends and so, after many a conversation over the backyard fence, **Gooseberry Patch** was born.

We put together our first catalog at our kitchen tables, enlisting the help of our loved ones wherever we could. From that very first mailing, we found an immediate connection with many of our customers and it wasn't long before we began receiving letters, photos and recipes from these new friends. In 1992, we put together our very first cookbook, compiled from hundreds of these recipes and, the rest, as they say, is history.

Hard to believe it's been 40 years since those kitchen-table days! From that original little **Gooseberry Patch** family, we've grown to include an amazing group of creative folks who love cooking, decorating and creating as much as we do. Today, we're best known for our homestyle, family-friendly cookbooks, now recognized as national bestsellers.

One thing's for sure, we couldn't have done it without our friends all across the country. Each year, we're honored to turn thousands of your recipes into our collectible cookbooks. Our hope is that each book captures the stories and heart of all of you who have shared with us. Whether you've been with us since the beginning or are just discovering us, welcome to the **Gooseberry Patch** family!

Visit our website anytime
www.gooseberrypatch.com

Jo Ann & Vickie

1·800·854·6673